Ultimate Guide to 2024

Summer Olympics in Paris

A Comprehensive Details and Analysis of the Buildup to the Sports Games Events

Paul Hiyonder

ISBN: 9798872017615

Gain access to more quality books from this author.

Table of Contents

Dedication

In honor of the pursuit of excellence, this book is dedicated to the indomitable spirit of athletes worldwide who inspire us with their dedication, passion, and commitment to their craft.

Acknowledgment

I want to express my sincere gratitude to everyone who contributed to the making of this book. Special thanks to the athletes, whose incredible stories form the heart of these pages. Your dedication and achievements are truly inspiring.

I also extend my appreciation to the organizers, supporters, and everyone involved in the 2024 Summer Olympics. Your hard work and commitment make these events possible.

A heartfelt thank you to my readers for joining me on this book. Your interest and support mean the world. Cheers to the spirit of the Olympics and the stories that unite us all.

Foreword

I am delighted to pen down a few words for this incredible book about the 2024 Summer Olympics. As someone who knows Paul and shares the same enthusiasm for sports, I can't help but feel excited about the upcoming event.

This book, skillfully crafted by Paul Hiyonder, promises to take you on a captivating journey into the heart of the Olympic Games. With Paul's passion for storytelling and love for the Olympics, you're in for a treat. Get ready for the events building up to the Summer Olympics in 2024.

As we eagerly await the 2024 Summer Olympics, let Paul guide you through the anticipation, excitement, and the unfolding narratives that make this global event so special.

Enjoy the read and get ready to cheer for the athletes who will undoubtedly leave an indelible mark on the history of the 2024 Summer Olympics.

— Sarah Evergreen

Introduction

Get ready for the 2024 Summer Olympics in Paris – it's going to be a big, exciting event! Athletes from all around the world will come together to compete in different sports and show their best skills.

Let me ask what makes the Olympics special? like the mascots, symbols, talented athletes, beautiful games, or breaking of Olympics records? We'll also check out the sports – both the classics and the new ones added this time.

But it's not all cheers and celebration. Some serious issues like problems for workers, worries about safety, and arguments about Russian and Belarusian athletes joining the Games have caused some concerns. The decisions made by the International Olympic Committee (IOC) have people talking and have both supporters and critics.

This introduction is just the beginning. We're going to explore everything about the 2024 Summer Olympics, from the exciting sports to the tricky problems. Let's ride into and understand the story leading up to this big event and how it might affect the world of sports. *Allons-y!*

Chapter 1: Background of the 2024 Summer Olympics

In the world of sports where nations unite,

A tale of rings, colors bright,

Blue, yellow, black, and green,

With red, a vibrant, spirited sheen.

Olympic circles, a symbol so grand,

Interlocking, they proudly stand.

Each hue, a flag's proud embrace,

A global gathering, a jubilant space.

In Paris, where history unfolds,

Centennial stories, as time beholds.

A guidebook crafted, emotions stirred,

Join the journey, embrace each word.

For in these rings, a legacy told,

A century's journey, bold and bold.

In every page, the Olympics ignite,

Colors swirling, an anthem of light.

The 2024 Summer Olympics, set to take place in Paris, France, emerged from a bidding process that involved five candidate cities: Paris, Hamburg, Budapest, Rome, and Los Angeles. However, the journey to awarding Paris the hosting rights was marked by withdrawals, political uncertainties, and cost concerns.

Hamburg withdrew its bid in November 2015 after a referendum, and Rome followed suit in September 2016, citing fiscal difficulties. Budapest faced a similar fate in February 2017, withdrawing after a petition against the bid gained substantial support for a referendum. These withdrawals prompted the International Olympic Committee (IOC) to consider a dual selection for the 2024 and 2028 host cities.

The IOC proposed the simultaneous election of host cities in 2017, a proposition approved during an Extraordinary IOC Session in July of that year. This decision led to discussions between the LA 2024 and

Paris 2024 bid committees, determining which city would host each Games and the feasibility of selecting both host cities simultaneously.

Paris emerged as the preferred host for 2024, and on July 31, 2017, Los Angeles became the sole candidate for 2028. The 131st IOC Session in September 2017 ratified both decisions, officially designating Paris as the host for the 2024 Summer Olympics.

The host city election took place on September 13, 2017, during the 131st IOC Session in Lima, Peru. Paris secured unanimous votes, solidifying its position as the chosen host for the 2024 Summer Olympics.

Looking ahead, the majority of Olympic events are planned for the city of Paris and its metropolitan region, incorporating neighboring cities like Saint-Denis, Le Bourget, Nanterre, Versailles, and Vaires-sur-Marne. While most competitions will be in proximity to Paris, certain events will be hosted in other cities. Lille, situated 225 km away, will host the handball tournaments, and Marseille, 777 km from the host city, will accommodate sailing and some football games. Additionally, surfing events are anticipated in Teahupo'o village in French Polynesia, an overseas territory located 15, 716 km from Paris. Football matches will also unfold in Bordeaux, Décines-Charpieu, Nantes, Nice, and Saint-Étienne, cities that are home to Ligue 1 clubs.

The 2024 Summer Olympics promise to bring together athletes from around the world in the vibrant backdrop of Paris, showcasing not only athletic prowess but also the cultural richness and diversity that define this global event. As the city prepares to welcome participants and spectators alike, anticipation builds for an Olympic Games that will leave an enduring mark on the tapestry of sports history.

Chapter 2: Historical Context of the Olympic Games

The Olympic Games are a big symbol of sports, teamwork, and global friendship. Let's look back at their history and see how France has been an important part of it.

The story of the Olympics begins a really long time ago in ancient Greece, around 776 BCE. People from different Greek cities would gather to show off their strength and skills in events like running, wrestling, and chariot racing. These Games were a big deal, not just for sports but also for culture and religion, bringing Greek people together.

Now, fast forward to the late 1800s. People were getting interested in ancient ideas and staying fit. A French educator named Pierre de Coubertin loved the ancient Olympic Games so much that he wanted to bring them back. He worked hard to make the modern Olympics happen.

In 1896, the first modern Olympics took place in Athens, Greece. The goal was to promote understanding between countries, friendship, and fair competition. Many nations liked Coubertin's idea, and the Games became really popular.

France, where Coubertin was from, has a special connection to the Olympics. The country has taken part in every Summer and Winter Games. Paris, the capital of France, even hosted the Olympics in 1900 and 1924, showing how important the city is to the Games.

The 1900 Summer Olympics in Paris were special because they were the first of the new era. Athletes from 24 nations competed in various sports, from traditional ones like running and gymnastics to unusual ones like croquet and live pigeon shooting. France did really well, winning 111 medals, including 31 gold, showing how good they were at sports and how much they embraced the Olympic spirit.

Then, the Winter Games came into the picture in 1924, happening in Chamonix, a French town in the Alps. This made the Olympics even more diverse, featuring cold-weather sports like skiing and ice hockey. France's involvement in both Summer and Winter Games highlights its commitment to a broad and inclusive sporting culture.

As time went on, France became a powerhouse in sports like cycling and fencing. They have a whopping 910 Olympic medals, including 272 gold, putting them among the best-performing nations.

Cycling is a big part of French culture, and French cyclists have achieved a lot, from road cycling to BMX racing. Athletes like Martin Fourcade, with five gold medals in biathlon from 2010 to 2018, have made France proud.

Fencing is another strong suit for France, with precise and skilled fencers like Philippe Cattiau and Roger Ducret winning eight medals each.

Even in the Winter Olympics, France shines, especially in Alpine skiing. Jean-Claude Killy winning all three gold medals in 1968 and more recent successes like biathlete Quentin Fillon Maillet at Beijing 2022 show that France is a force to be reckoned with in winter sports.

France doesn't just excel in individual performances; it also takes the responsibility of hosting the Games seriously. Hosting five Olympics, including the 2024 Summer Games in Paris, shows France's dedication to the Olympic Movement. Next year's Olympics signify the centennial celebration of 1924 Olympics. It gonna be lit, I believe!

The history of the Olympic Games is closely connected to France's sports legacy. From the early days of the modern Olympics to today, France has consistently shown its commitment to the Games. As we celebrate the victories and diversity of the Olympic Movement, France stands out as a symbol of sporting excellence, unity, and the enduring spirit of the Games.

2.1 **Host Country: France**

When a country hosts the Olympics, it means they have a big responsibility. It's not just about having places for sports; it's a special time when the whole world looks at that country for sports, sharing culture, and coming together.

To be a host country, you need to plan carefully and build things like stadiums. France, with its long history and beautiful places, chose special venues. For example, they picked the famous Roland-Garros Stadium for tennis and boxing and the stunning Château de Versailles for equestrian and modern pentathlon events. Each place adds something unique to the Olympics.

Being the host puts France in the spotlight globally, not just for sports but also for its culture. The Olympics let France show its history, arts, and delicious food. Famous places like the Eiffel Tower and Place de la Concorde aren't just backgrounds for sports; they also host cultural events and celebrations.

Hosting the Olympics can bring a lot of money to a country. Even though building things initially costs a lot, in the long run, it's usually worth it. More people come to visit, the media talks about the country, and tourism increases. For France, which is already known for being a great place to visit, hosting the Olympics is a chance to attract even more people and help the economy grow.

Beyond money, hosting the Olympics leaves a positive impact on the community. People get inspired to do sports and live a healthier life. The new sports facilities built or improved for the Games become useful for many years. France shows its commitment to making a good impact, not only in Paris and nearby places but also in faraway territories like Tahiti, where surfing events will take place.

On the world stage, hosting the Olympics lets the country contribute to the Olympic ideals of unity, friendship, and peace. By inviting athletes from all over, France helps create a sense of togetherness that goes beyond borders. The Games become a chance for countries to understand and cooperate with each other.

Being the host country for the Olympics is a big job that goes beyond just sports. For France, it's a special time to share its history, culture, and love for sportsmanship. From carefully chosen venues to cultural events and economic benefits, France hosting the Olympics shows the spirit of unity, diversity, and the pursuit of excellence.

2.2 **Host City: Paris**

Choosing a city to host the Olympics is a big deal, way more than just figuring out where to put the events. Paris is the chosen city this time, and it brings a lot to the table – history, culture, and a strong commitment to being excellent.

Paris isn't just a place for sports; it's known as the "City of Light" because it's been a center of smart and artistic thinking for a really long time. With a history dating back from the Renaissance to the Enlightenment, Paris is a symbol of human progress. Picking Paris as the Olympics host shows how important its history is to the world.

Paris is full of famous buildings like the Eiffel Tower and Notre-Dame Cathedral. Now, these historic spots are turning into places for the Olympic games. It's not just about sports; it's like blending athletic competitions with the cool history of Paris, creating a unique and beautiful show that goes beyond normal sports events.

More than just monuments, Paris is a hub for culture, literature, art, and philosophy. Places like the Louvre, home to the Mona Lisa, and the Musée d'Orsay, full of Impressionist art, aren't just museums – they're becoming part of the Olympic experience. They'll host events, exhibitions, and celebrations that mix art and sports in a special Olympic celebration.

Paris is also making a big effort to be eco-friendly and innovative. They're into green ideas like environmentally friendly transportation and sustainable venues. It's not just about showing off sports skills; Paris wants to set an example for future Olympic hosts on how to take care of the environment.

The impact of Paris hosting the Olympics goes beyond just the money they make during the Games. More people visiting, the whole world watching on TV, and Paris being shown as a top tourist spot all add up to lasting economic benefits. The Olympics become a rcason for more people to visit, boosting Paris's reputation as a big cultural and economic player.

For the people living in Paris, hosting the Olympics is a big deal socially too. They're investing in sports places and encouraging a healthy lifestyle. The new or improved sports facilities aren't just for the Games; they're becoming community places for people to enjoy sports and fun long after the Olympics are over.

Paris as the Olympics host is like bringing together history, culture, and modern values. It turns the city into a world stage where sports and art meet, blending the past with future dreams. Paris, with its timeless charm and strong commitment to being the best, is all set to create an Olympic experience that goes way beyond just sports – it's a celebration of what people can achieve together.

2.3 **Venues at the 2024 Olympics in France**

The 2024 Olympic Games in France are set to showcase a spectacular array of venues, each contributing to the unique tapestry of this global sporting event. These venues, spread across Paris and the surrounding Ile-de-France region, as well as select locations outside mainland France, promise not only thrilling athletic competitions but also a celebration of the rich cultural and historical heritage.

Paris Centre Venues:
The heart of Paris will pulsate with sporting energy as iconic locations take center stage. Roland-Garros Stadium, renowned for hosting the French Open, will witness intense boxing and tennis competitions. The historic Parc des Princes, home to football club Paris Saint-Germain, will resonate with the cheers of soccer enthusiasts. The Eiffel Tower Stadium, nestled in the Champs de Mars, will transform into a captivating backdrop for beach volleyball matches, judo, and wrestling.

The Champ de Mars Arena, positioned opposite the École Militaire, will host gripping judo and wrestling competitions, while athletes in urban sports like BMX Freestyle, Skateboarding, 3×3 Basketball, and Breaking will showcase their skills at the iconic Place de la Concorde. The Grand Palais, with its awe-inspiring glass roof, will be a fitting venue for fencing and taekwondo, adding a touch of elegance to the Games.

Ile-de-France Venues:

Venturing into the Ile-de-France region unveils a diverse array of venues. Elancourt Hill will echo with the excitement of mountain biking, while the Saint-Quentin-en-Yvelines Velodrome will host thrilling cycling events. The stunning Château de Versailles, a UNESCO World Heritage site, will provide a majestic setting for equestrian and modern pentathlon competitions.

Paris La Défense Arena, a multi-purpose venue, will witness the prowess of swimmers and water polo players. Yves-du-Manoir Stadium, steeped in history as the primary arena for the Paris 1924 Olympics, will once again be the stage for hockey competitions, highlighting its enduring significance.

Outside Venues:

The 2024 Olympics transcend mainland France, reaching out to diverse locations. In Marseille, the Stade Vélodrome, home to Olympique de Marseille, will host football matches, while the Marseille Marina will welcome sailing events. The picturesque Teahupo'o in Tahiti, an overseas collectivity of France, will make history by hosting the Olympic surfing competition on its renowned waves.

From the grandeur of Parisian landmarks to the serene landscapes of Versailles and the exhilarating waves of Teahupo'o, the 2024 Olympics promise a journey through both time and space, uniting athletes and spectators in the spirit of global celebration.

These carefully chosen venues not only symbolize the essence of each sport but also reflect the commitment to accessibility and convenience for participants and attendees. As the countdown to the Games continues, anticipation builds for the moments of triumph and the shared experiences that will unfold in these remarkable venues, leaving an indelible mark on the legacy of the 2024 Olympics in France.

2.4 **Emblems and Mascots**

Emblems and mascots play a significant role in shaping the identity and spirit of major sporting events like the Olympics. The 2024 Summer Olympics and Paralympics in Paris are no exception, featuring a distinct emblem and mascots that capture the essence of the games.

Emblem:

The emblem, unveiled on October 21, 2019, draws inspiration from Art Deco and represents Marianne, the national personification of France. What stands out is the clever use of negative space in Marianne's hair to form a flame, symbolizing the power and magic of the Games. Additionally, the emblem bears a resemblance to a gold medal, reinforcing the competitive and celebratory nature of the event. Designed by Sylvain Boyer with the collaboration of French design agencies, the emblem pays homage to the 1900 Summer Olympics in Paris, where women were first allowed to participate.

The emblem's design received both praise and some mockery on social media, showcasing the subjective nature of artistic interpretation. A survey indicated a high approval rating among the French population, with more than 80% expressing their liking for the emblem. It is interesting to note the emblem's connection to the historical context of the Games, reflecting the evolving cultural and social dynamics.

Mascots:
The mascots for the 2024 Olympics and Paralympics, known as The Phryges, were revealed on November 14,

2022. These anthropomorphic Phrygian caps hold historical significance in French symbolism, representing freedom and liberty. The choice of mascots aligns with Marianne's common depiction wearing the Phrygian cap in various artworks, including Eugène Delacroix's painting, signifying liberty and democracy. The motto, "Alone we go faster, but together we go further," emphasizes unity and collaboration, essential elements in both sports and society.

The decision to have the same emblem for both the Olympics and Paralympics reflects a shared ambition and inclusivity between the two events. This marks a departure from the traditional approach of having distinct emblems for the Olympics and Paralympics, symbolizing a unified celebration of athletic achievement.

Emblems and mascots serve as visual representations that go beyond mere symbols. They become a cultural bridge, connecting the past, present, and future of the host nation and the global community. The Paris 2024 emblems and mascots carry the spirit of inclusivity, historical homage, and the shared journey of athletes and spectators alike.

Chapter 3: Sports Programme

Paris is getting ready for the Olympics, featuring a variety of sports throughout the city and nearby areas. The well-known Stade de France will host athletics, rugby, and the closing ceremony, while the nearby Aquatics Centre will be the hub for water sports.

There are 28 core Olympic sports, including archery, athletics, basketball, boxing, cycling, equestrian, football, gymnastics, judo, rowing, sailing, swimming, weightlifting, and wrestling. Additionally, four more sports, breaking, sport climbing, skateboarding, and surfing, will add a lively touch to the Games.

Different venues have specific sports. In 2024, Trocadéro ensures a remarkable vantage point and immersive experience for viewers, both on-site and watching on television, during the road cycling and 20km race walk events in athletics. In this historic

Olympic moment, men and women will compete on the same route for their time trials for the first time.

Bercy Arena will showcase basketball, artistic gymnastics, and trampoline, while the Eiffel Tower Stadium will be the venue for beach volleyball. The Grand Palais will host fencing and taekwondo, and La Chapelle Arena will feature badminton and rhythmic gymnastics. The Invalides venue will highlight archery and marathon athletics, and La Concorde Stadium will be the location for 3×3 basketball, BMX freestyle, breaking, and skateboard events.

Other notable locations include Parc des Princes for football, Pont Alexandre III for marathon swimming, cycling road, and triathlon, and Roland Garros Stadium for boxing and tennis. Various arenas will cater to handball, table tennis, volleyball, and weightlifting. The Aquatic Centre will host artistic swimming, diving, and water polo. Château de Versailles will be the setting for equestrian events, while Le Bourget will showcase sport climbing. Vaires-Sur-Marne Nautic Stadium will be the venue for canoe slalom, canoe sprint, and rowing, and Saint-Quentin-en-Yvelines Velodrome will host track cycling.

Paris 2024 promises a diverse range of sports spread across iconic venues, creating a lively and inclusive Olympic experience.

3.1 Introducing New Sports at the 2024 Paris Olympics: A Wave of Freshness

The 2024 Paris Olympics are gearing up to make history not only with their picturesque setting along the Seine River but also by introducing a host of exciting new developments. Beyond the iconic landmarks and the 50/50 male-female ratio, one of the most anticipated aspects is the inclusion of several novel sports, adding a contemporary flair to the traditional Olympic lineup.

Olympic Skateboarding: A Street and Park Extravaganza

Skateboarding, once the emblem of urban youth culture, is set to take center stage as one of the new Olympic sports at Paris 2024. The International Olympic Committee (IOC) acknowledged the immense popularity of skateboarding, especially among the younger generation, leading to its inclusion as an official Olympic sport starting from Tokyo 2020. In Paris, the skateboarding events will showcase both male and female competitors, with competitions unfolding on the streets and in specially designed parks. The inclusion of skateboarding not only reflects the evolving interests of the youth but also emphasizes the Olympics' commitment to staying relevant and engaging.

Olympic Sport Climbing: Scaling New Heights

While climbing already made its mark at the Tokyo 2020 Olympics, Paris 2024 is set to continue the ascent of this exhilarating sport. Olympic sport climbing comprises three distinct disciplines: Speed, challenging athletes to climb at breakneck pace; Bouldering, testing skills on climbing boulders; and Lead, pushing climbers up a daunting 20-meter route. The fusion of tactics, insight, agility, strength, and endurance makes sport climbing a captivating addition to the Olympic program. Its inclusion not only adds a layer of diversity but also invites athletes to master a range of climbing challenges, showcasing the versatility of the human spirit.

Olympic Surfing: A Pacific Wave in Paris

Despite the landlocked location of Paris, Olympic surfing promises a unique and distant adventure. The surf competitions will unfold on the captivating waves of Teahupoo, located on the island of Tahiti in French Polynesia. This geographical juxtaposition adds a touch of exoticism to the Paris Olympics, bridging the continents and showcasing the universal appeal of surfing. While the athletes may not ride the Seine, the inclusion of Olympic surfing represents a nod to the global nature of the Games and the celebration of sports beyond geographical confines.

Olympic Breakdancing: Dancing into Olympic History

Breaking, the dynamic and expressive dance form that originated in urban cultures, is set to make its Olympic debut in Paris 2024. This addition brings a unique challenge to the Olympics – how to evaluate a discipline rooted in artistic freedom. Only four athletes per continent will have the opportunity to showcase their breakdancing prowess on this prestigious stage. The judging criteria, centered around creativity and musicality, adds a layer of subjectivity that aligns with the fluid and expressive nature of breakdancing. This new Olympic sport not only celebrates diversity in movement but also opens the door for unconventional and artistic expressions to shine on the Olympic stage.

The introduction of these new sports at the 2024 Paris Olympics signifies more than just a change in the event lineup. It embodies a commitment to embracing the dynamic interests of the global audience, recognizing the cultural richness of sports, and fostering a sense of inclusivity that transcends borders. As the world eagerly awaits the spectacle along the Seine, the waves of change brought by these new sports promise to make the Paris Olympics a memorable and groundbreaking chapter in the history of the Games.

3.2 Core and Optional Sports

The Paris 2024 Summer Olympics will have both traditional and new sports. The International Olympic Committee (IOC) made rules in 2017, and the Games will include 28 core sports from the 2016 program, with up to six optional sports for variety.

In September 2017, during the 131st IOC Session, the 28 sports from 2016 got approval for Paris 2024. The Paris Organising Committee could suggest up to five extra sports, and in February 2019, it proposed optional sports like breakdancing, skateboarding, sport climbing, and surfing. These sports, part of the 2020 Summer Olympics for the first time, got approval in June 2019.

Paris 2024 is special as the first Summer Olympics since 1960 with fewer events than the previous one, featuring 32 sports and 329 events. A significant change is adding breaking as a new discipline with two events. Sport climbing changed too, with the previous 'combined' event now split into speed climbing and boulder-and-lead for each gender.

The four extra sports proposed by Paris 2024, breaking, sport climbing, skateboarding, and surfing, each bring something unique. Aligned with the IOC's vision for inclusive, gender-balanced, and youth-centered games, Paris 2024 used the chance in the Olympic Agenda 2020 to enhance its program, focusing on inclusivity and youth appeal.

The IOC confirmed the event program, athlete quotas, and the inclusion of these new sports in December 2020, showing a commitment to creativity and athletic performance. Breaking, sport climbing, skateboarding, and surfing, known for their accessibility and vibrant communities on social media, are set to inspire millions of children to take up sports in the next five years.

As the world looks forward to this global sporting event, including these sports not only makes the Olympic experience richer but also connects with the changing interests of a new generation of athletes and fans.

3.3 **Evolution of Events at the 2024 Paris Olympics**

The upcoming 2024 Paris Olympics bring a wave of changes and exciting developments to the world of sports. These alterations in events not only reflect a dynamic shift in the sporting landscape but also cater to evolving interests and preferences.

Adaptations in Core Sports:

Traditionally established sports, often referred to as core sports, are not immune to change. While preserving their fundamental essence, these sports undergo modifications to stay relevant and engaging. For instance, track and field events, a staple of the Olympics, may see tweaks in formats or the introduction of new disciplines. These adaptations aim to enhance the spectator experience and provide athletes with fresh challenges, ensuring the longevity and vibrancy of these time-honored competitions.

Introduction of Innovative Disciplines:

The 2024 Paris Olympics mark the introduction of innovative disciplines, injecting a dose of novelty into the Games. Sports like surfing, skateboarding, and sport climbing, categorized as optional sports, represent this wave of innovation. These disciplines, often popular among younger audiences, bring a contemporary flair to the Olympics. By embracing these new additions, the Games expand their appeal to a broader demographic and reflect the ever-changing landscape of global sporting interests.

Technological Advancements in Sports:

Beyond changes in specific events, technology plays a pivotal role in shaping the future of sports. From advanced equipment to data analytics, athletes benefit from cutting-edge innovations that push the boundaries of performance. The integration of technology not only elevates the level of competition but also provides a platform for athletes to showcase their skills in innovative ways. This technological evolution contributes to the overall modernization of the Olympic Games.

Emphasis on Inclusivity and Diversity:

The changes in events at the 2024 Paris Olympics underscore a commitment to inclusivity and diversity. The inclusion of sports with diverse cultural roots and global popularity reflects a desire to make the Games more representative of the world's sporting landscape. This emphasis on inclusivity ensures that athletes from various backgrounds and regions have the opportunity to showcase their talents on the grand stage, fostering a sense of unity through sport.

Balancing Tradition and Progress:

While embracing changes, the organizers of the 2024 Paris Olympics strive to strike a balance between tradition and progress. The evolution of events acknowledges the rich history of the Games while embracing the need for innovation. This delicate equilibrium ensures that the Olympics remain a timeless celebration of athletic excellence while adapting to the ever-evolving tastes and expectations of a global audience.

The changes in events at the 2024 Paris Olympics reflect a dynamic and forward-thinking approach to sports. Whether through adaptations in core sports, the introduction of innovative disciplines, technological advancements, or a commitment to inclusivity, these changes contribute to the continued evolution and excitement of the Olympic Games.

Chapter 4: Athlete Count by Country

The list of National Olympic Committees participating in the 2024 Olympics is quite extensive and showcases a global representation of countries with at least one qualified athlete. As of December 12, these nations, numbering from Albania to Zimbabwe, bring a rich diversity of cultures, talents, and sporting prowess to the forefront of the international stage.

From the African continent, countries like Algeria, Angola, and Nigeria have made significant contributions, qualifying athletes across various disciplines. Moving across the Atlantic, nations such as Argentina, Brazil, and Canada are set to display their athletic excellence.

Europe, with its rich sporting tradition, is well-represented by countries like France, host to the event with an impressive contingent of 434 athletes, along with Germany, Great Britain, and the Netherlands. The Asian continent contributes significantly, with China, Japan, and South Korea showcasing their prowess in various sports.

The Middle East, represented by countries like Egypt, Israel, and the United Arab Emirates, adds its unique flavor to the Olympic mix. Oceania, with Australia and New Zealand leading the charge, brings a strong presence from the Southern Hemisphere.

Individual Neutral Athletes, numbering 11, signify a unique aspect of the Olympics, allowing athletes to compete independently of a specific national affiliation.

The numerical breakdown of athletes by country further emphasizes the scale of participation. France, as the host, leads with 434 athletes, closely followed by the United States with 399. Australia, China, and Great Britain complete the top five in terms of athlete representation.

This diverse assembly of National Olympic Committees not only reflects the universal appeal of the Olympics but also highlights the unifying power of sports on a global scale. As these nations come together, the 2024 Olympics promise to be a celebration of talent, sportsmanship, and the spirit of international camaraderie.

Chapter 5: Challenges and Controversies

The road to the 2024 Summer Olympics in Paris is not without its challenges and controversies. With less than nine months remaining until the grand opening ceremony, the host city is grappling with various issues that demand attention and resolution.

One contentious matter revolves around the ban on bouquinistes, the traditional booksellers who have been a part of the Parisian landscape since the 16th century. Authorities aim to eliminate street vending, fortune-telling, and other activities deemed delinquent. This move, however, has sparked debate as it includes the expulsion of the historic bouquinistes. Concerns over potential security threats, particularly during the crowded opening ceremony along the Seine River, have led to the decision.

Another pressing concern is the situation of homelessness in Paris. The French government, although asserting that it is unrelated to the upcoming Olympics, has expedited plans to relocate homeless individuals from the city streets to other French cities. This initiative, affecting approximately half of France's homeless population, aims to offer better job prospects, access to charities, and reconnection with family and friends. However, the decision of some hotels to cancel emergency housing contracts has added complexity to the issue, raising questions about the city's preparedness for the anticipated influx of tourists.

Paris also faces a bedbug panic, with reports of an increase in infestations, particularly during the summer. The issue not only poses hygienic concerns but also raises worries about the psychological impact and potential damage to the city's image in the lead-up to the Olympics. The organizers are keen to ensure that the new Olympic Village in Seine-Saint-Denis remains free of such issues, emphasizing sustainability and environmental friendliness.

Furthermore, the debate over hijabs and secularism has resurfaced as the Olympics approach. While France prohibits its athletes from wearing head coverings, the International Olympic Committee permits athletes to wear veils in the Olympic Village, leaving the decision to each sport's federation. This has reignited discussions about religious symbols in French public life, given the country's constitutional commitment to secularism.

The challenges extend beyond the physical and social aspects. Financial prosecutors raided the Paris 2024 Olympics headquarters, targeting event management firms, as part of an investigation into suspected illegal activities related to contract awards. Additionally, a digital interference campaign originating from Azerbaijan sought to undermine confidence in France's ability to organize the Games, threatening a boycott.

Paris grapples with a myriad of challenges and controversies on its journey to hosting the 2024 Summer Olympics. The city's ability to address and overcome these issues will play a crucial role in shaping the success and legacy of the upcoming Games.

Chapter 6: Olympics Torch

This torch is beautiful!

The Paris 2024 Olympics Torch is more than just a flame carrier; it's a symbol of togetherness. Designed by Mathieu Lehanneur, it takes inspiration from Equality, Water, and Peacefulness. The torch's special champagne color represents the spirit of the upcoming Games and holds a meaningful message.

Created for both the Olympic and Paralympic Games, the torch signifies a commitment to fairness. It has perfect symmetry, showing that equal effort is put into organizing both events. Paris 2024 proudly stands as the first Olympic Games with an equal number of male and female participants.

Water, a vital element for Paris 2024, is beautifully incorporated into the torch's design. From the flame's journey across the Mediterranean to reaching distant oceans, the torch symbolizes the flowing nature of water. The iconic River Seine is also part of its inspiration.

Peacefulness, a crucial aspect of the Olympics, is reflected in the torch's gentle curves. It aims to capture the calm and harmonious spirit of the Games.

The torch's journey is as remarkable as its design. It begins with the flame being lit in Olympia, Greece, using sunlight reflected off a parabolic mirror—a tribute to the strength of the Greek god Apollo. Carried by about 10, 000 torchbearers, it travels from Greece to Marseille, arriving on May 8, 2024. Then, it embarks on a 68-day journey across 65 French territories before lighting the Olympic cauldron in Paris on July 26, 2024. After the Olympic Games, the torch is reignited in Stoke Mandeville, symbolizing the Paralympic Games' home, for a new relay leading to the Paralympic Games' Opening Ceremony on August 28, 2024.

The torch's physical features add to its importance. Weighing 1. 5kg and standing at 70cm, it's made of 100% recycled ArcelorMittal XCarb® steel. This aligns with Paris 2024's goal for sustainability. The torch's wavy touch, representing the Mediterranean Sea, adds a special touch.

Production is a careful process, melting six tons of recycled steel, laser-cutting, welding, and assembling it by skilled workers. The torch is designed to be wind and waterproof, tested against a three-meter fall, ensuring its resilience during the relay.

This torch, with its simple yet powerful symbolism, is more than a ceremonial item; it's a piece of history embodying the values and dreams of the Paris 2024 Olympics. As it travels through the hands of torchbearers and across diverse landscapes, it becomes a uniting force, connecting people through the shared spirit of the Games.

Chapter 7: Budget for 2024 Olympics

The financial journey of the Paris 2024 Olympics has been marked by a series of challenges and strategic decisions aimed at ensuring a balanced budget. Facing headwinds such as inflation, security concerns, and the quest for financial partners, the organizers have navigated a path to fiscal responsibility.

The budget, initially set at €4 billion, saw an increase of €400 million, reaching a total of €4. 38 billion. This decision, approved by the Paris 2024 board, represents a 10% boost and followed a rigorous process of collaboration between the organizing committee, the International Olympic Committee (IOC), and stakeholders.

A key focus has been on prudent financial management, given the historical challenges faced by previous Olympic Games that led to financial strains. The audit committee, established in 2018, cautioned that planned expenditures were surpassing expected revenues. In response, the organizers sought ways to cut costs across various budget lines, streamline specifications, and optimize venue capacities.

The revised budget takes into account changes in the cost of delivering the Games, with a contingency reserve maintained at €200 million. This reserve acts as a protective measure to cover unforeseen circumstances and risks. Paris 2024 emphasizes its commitment to avoiding a reliance on public funds, with private funding constituting 96% of the financing.

Revenue generation has been a crucial aspect of financial stability. Paris 2024 claims to have reached 80% of its revenue target by the end of 2022. The organizers achieved this through increased income projections from domestic partnerships and successful ticket sales. Notably, public funding for the Paralympics received a boost, with contributions from entities like the French

State, Métropole du Grand Paris, City of Paris, and Ile-de-France Region.

As of July 18, 2023, the operating budget for the Paris Olympics is declared being monitored. The president of the organizing committee, Tony Estanguet, highlighted the unprecedented achievement of raising over €1 billion from private partnerships. Negotiations for additional partnerships, including a potential deal with luxury group LVMH, are in progress.

The overall budget for the Paris Olympics, encompassing venue construction and renovation costs, is approximately €8 billion. Beyond the financial aspects, the organizers are focused on creating a lasting legacy. Initiatives like Club Paris 2024, Terre de Jeux 2024, and Génération 2024 aim to have a long-term impact. The commitment to a circular economy and anticipation as a central strategy for physical legacy reinforces the goal of sustainable outcomes.

The ongoing dialogue about hosting the 2030 Winter Olympics in the French Alps further extends the potential impact of Paris 2024's programs. The agreement on the subsequent dissolution of the Organizing Committee, formalizing plans for each venue and providing support for employees transitioning post-Games, reflects a structured approach to the event's conclusion.

The financial journey of the Paris 2024 Olympics highlights the delicate balance between ambitious goals, cost management, and ensuring a lasting legacy that extends beyond the Olympic year.

Chapter 8: IOC Decisions on Russian and Belarusian Athletes

The participation of Russian and Belarusian athletes in the 2024 Olympics has sparked significant debate and decisions from the International Olympic Committee (IOC). The controversy arose due to the Russian invasion of Ukraine, leading to discussions on whether these athletes should compete and, if so, under what conditions.

In February 2022, the IOC recommended sports federations to ban Russian and Belarusian athletes from international tournaments, citing the violation of the Olympic Truce. This recommendation triggered concerns about the potential financial and political impact of allowing these athletes to participate.

In January 2023, the IOC announced plans to introduce Russian and Belarusian athletes as neutrals. This decision, aimed at avoiding a complete exclusion, was met with mixed reactions. Poland's sport and tourism minister expressed concerns, stating that up to 40 countries might consider boycotting the 2024 Olympics if Russian and Belarusian athletes were not excluded.

Various nations, including Denmark, Estonia, Latvia, Lithuania, Poland, and Ukraine, voiced their intentions to potentially boycott the Games. Speculation also surrounded the United Kingdom, Canada, Japan, New Zealand, and South Korea regarding a boycott.

The United Nations released a report in February 2023 commending the IOC for considering reinstating Russian and Belarusian athletes but urged further steps to ensure athletes aren't forced to take sides in the conflict. The UN emphasized the importance of aligning recommendations with international human rights standards.

While some countries welcomed the return of these athletes under certain conditions, others, like the Czech

Republic and Greece, opposed the idea of a boycott. Australia and Germany indicated they would welcome Russia, albeit reluctantly.

IOC President Thomas Bach emphasized that decisions about athlete participation should not be left to national governments, opposing the notion of collective guilt for Russian and Belarusian athletes. The IOC supported the return of these athletes under specific conditions, excluding national symbols and organizations.

Despite IOC and UN statements supporting the return of Russian and Belarusian athletes, Ukrainian officials expressed dissatisfaction, accusing them of appeasing Russia. The Association of National Olympic Committees of Africa endorsed the IOC's decision to reinstate these athletes.

In March 2023, the International Fencing Federation became the first Olympic governing body to officially reinstate Russian and Belarusian athletes, leading to protests and event cancellations by some countries.

As of July 2023, the IOC stated that Russia and Belarus would not be formally invited, but their athletes could compete as neutrals, a decision later confirmed in December 2023. The IOC addressed accusations of double standards regarding Israel, clarifying that different circumstances surrounded Israel's actions in Gaza.

The IOC's decisions regarding the participation of Russian and Belarusian athletes in the 2024 Olympics reflect the complexities of navigating geopolitical tensions and maintaining the purpose of unity. The process involved careful considerations, responses to global opinions, and efforts to find a middle ground that allows athletes to compete while addressing international concerns.

8.1 Conditions for Participation

The participation conditions for Russian and Belarusian athletes in the upcoming Paris 2024 Olympics have undergone a series of developments, reflecting the complexities surrounding the geopolitical space. Initially facing bans from international sports events following Russia's invasion of Ukraine, the athletes are now permitted to compete as "Individual Neutral Athletes" (INAs) in the Paris Games.

The International Olympic Committee (IOC) decided on this unique status, allowing qualifying athletes to participate without displaying national flags, emblems, or anthems. This decision, confirmed in December 2023, stirred both criticism and support. Athletes from these countries can only compete in individual sports, with no representation in team sports. Additionally, no Russian or Belarusian government or state officials will be invited or accredited for Paris 2024.

To be eligible as INAs, athletes must have qualified through existing qualification systems of International Federations (IFs) and must adhere to strict criteria.

Those actively supporting the war in Ukraine or contracted to the Russian or Belarusian military are ineligible.

The IOC's decision marked a shift from the initial ban, with some sports federations reinstating Russian and Belarusian athletes. The eligibility conditions aim to balance the inclusion of individual athletes with addressing geopolitical concerns. The IOC faced criticism from Ukraine for allowing these athletes to participate, emphasizing potential discrimination against Ukrainian competitors.

The dilemma faced by the IOC is evident, navigating between geopolitical tensions and maintaining the principles of international sports.

As the Paris 2024 Olympics approach, the conditions set by the IOC for Russian and Belarusian athletes reflect a delicate balance between inclusivity, political considerations, and the desire to uphold the integrity of international sports competitions. The evolving nature of these conditions underscores the challenges faced by sports organizations in navigating complex geopolitical scenarios.

8.2 **Backlash and Reactions**

The recent decision by the International Olympic Committee (IOC) to allow Russian and Belarusian athletes to participate in the 2024 Paris Olympic Games as neutrals has triggered significant backlash and a variety of reactions from different quarters.

One of the most vocal critics has been Ukraine, whose foreign affairs minister, Dmytro Kuleba, expressed strong condemnation on social media. Kuleba argued that the IOC's decision essentially gives Russia the opportunity to weaponize the Olympics for propaganda warfare. He urged all partners to strongly condemn what he described as a shameful decision undermining Olympic principles. President Volodymyr Zelenskyy and other Ukrainian officials had consistently called for the outright ban of Russian and Belarusian athletes from the Games, emphasizing Russia's actions as incompatible with the values of the civilized world.

Russia, on the other hand, maintains that forcing their athletes to compete as neutrals is discriminatory and damaging to the Olympic Games itself. Oleg Matytsin, Russia's sports minister, criticized the decision, claiming it goes against the principles of sport. This reflects the ongoing tension between the involved parties regarding the treatment of Russian and Belarusian athletes in the wake of geopolitical events.

The Baltic presidents, including those from Lithuania, Latvia, and Estonia, expressed disappointment and disagreement with the IOC's decision. President Alar Karis of Estonia called the decision unacceptable, both as a citizen and a sports enthusiast. Lithuanian President Gitanas Nauseda labeled the decision as displeasing and emphasized that Olympic principles should not align with acts of terror, murder, or destruction.

The decision has also sparked reactions on social media platforms, with individuals expressing strong opinions. Some call for a potential boycott of the Paris Olympics, arguing that allowing Russian athletes to compete as neutrals compromises the values and integrity of the Games. Comparisons to historical boycotts, such as the 1980 Moscow Games, have been invoked, highlighting the potential impact of collective actions against the decision.

The controversy surrounding the IOC's decision sheds light on the intersection of sports and geopolitics, raising questions about the role of international sports organizations in navigating complex global issues. The reactions underscore the challenges faced by such organizations in maintaining the principles of fair play while grappling with the broader political landscape. As the situation unfolds, the Olympic Games in Paris become a focal point for discussions on ethics, neutrality, and the role of sports in times of geopolitical turmoil.

8.3 IOC's Decision and Its Implications

The IOC's decision to let Russian and Belarusian athletes compete as neutrals in the 2024 Paris Olympics has sent shockwaves through the world of sports, geopolitics, and ethics. This choice, made against the backdrop of the devastating Russian invasion of Ukraine, is not just a sports decision; it's a statement that goes beyond the playing field.

One of the most significant impacts is the diplomatic fallout. It's hard to separate sports and politics, especially when athletes from countries involved in a conflict are allowed to participate as if everything is normal. Ukraine's Foreign Affairs Minister, Dmytro Kuleba, didn't mince words, stating that the IOC essentially gave Russia the green light to use the Olympics for propaganda. This turns the Games into more than a celebration of athleticism; it becomes a stage for political tensions.

The ethical considerations are hard-hitting. Critics argue that the IOC's decision compromises the very essence of the Olympic Games. Neutrality in the face of real-world conflict and human rights abuses raises questions about the moral compass of international sports organizations. Is it right to maintain neutrality when a participating country's actions directly contradict the spirit of the Olympics?

The decision's selective nature introduces a complex layer. Allowing individual athletes but not teams reflects a cautious approach, an attempt to balance inclusion with avoiding perceived endorsement of the countries' actions. It's a delicate dance between letting athletes compete and avoiding a collective representation that might be seen as condoning wrongdoing.

Social media is buzzing with dissatisfaction and calls for potential boycotts, showcasing the broader societal impact. People are emotionally invested, expressing their frustration and disappointment. Comparisons to historical boycotts, like the 1980 Moscow Games, highlight the symbolic power of such actions and underline sports' potential as a platform for meaningful protest.

Looking ahead, the IOC's decision sets a precedent with far-reaching consequences. The world will be watching how sports organizations solve this problem. The Paris Olympics in 2024 will be more than a sports spectacle; they will be a stage for discussions on sportsmanship, diplomacy, and ethics. The implications of this decision will continue to reverberate, sparking emotional discussions in a world grappling with the harsh realities of geopolitical challenges.

Chapter 9: The beauty of Olympics village at Paris 2024

Over the past 100 years, the Olympic Village has changed a lot. It started in 1924 in Paris with small wooden huts for athletes, and now it's a symbol of togetherness at the Games.

Looking ahead to the Paris 2024 Olympics, they're building the Olympic Village in Seine-Saint-Denis, the poorest area in mainland France. SOLIDEO is in charge, and they promise the village will leave a positive impact. After the Games, it will turn into a neighborhood for 6, 000 people, with offices, shops, cultural spots, schools, and a park.

They chose Saint-Denis Pleyel for the Olympic Village because it fits the goals for sustainability and making money. This area, with the Stade de France and Cité du

Cinéma, keeps changing, showing how important it is to adapt to the surroundings.

The Olympic Village isn't just a place to stay; it's where athletes from 205 nations and the IOC Refugee Olympic Team meet. Henri Specht, who oversees the project, opines that part of the Games is lost when there is no Olympic Village.

Paris 2024 isn't just about hosting athletes; it's about making a long-term impact on the local community. The Olympic Village, close to the Stade de France, will have green spaces, like a public park, helping the area grow even after the Games.

As the Village gets ready, it's not just for 2024; a year later, it opens for 6, 000 residents, showing how it'll keep benefiting the host city. The Olympic Village changing over time shows a commitment to being eco-friendly, involving the community, and having a plan that goes beyond the Games.

9.1 **Official Motto**

The official motto for the Olympic and Paralympic Games Paris 2024 is "Games Wide Open." This phrase embodies the overarching spirit and goals of the global sporting event. Unveiled during the two-year countdown celebrations, the motto reflects the ambition, inclusivity, and transformative vision of the organizers.

"Games Wide Open" invites the world to collectively embrace new experiences and emotions. This ambition extends beyond the sports arena to create a platform for shared thrills, unique disciplines, and outdoor competitions in the heart of Paris.

The power of the motto goes beyond the physical aspects of sports, signifying the ability to open hearts and minds, fostering unity between non-disabled athletes and Para athletes, as well as across genders. The French team is envisioned as a single entity, emphasizing inclusion and parity between the Olympic and Paralympic Games.

Highlighting the transformative power of sports, the idea of opening the emotions of sport reflects the belief that sports can unite, break down barriers, and celebrate diversity. The ambition extends to writing a collective story spanning generations, welcoming contributions from all territories and individuals.

The concept of opening the Games to all energies symbolizes Paris 2024's dream as a catalyst for societal transformation, particularly in Seine-Saint-Denis. The ambition is to create groundbreaking Games that imagine the world of tomorrow, testing, inventing, creating, and providing solutions that genuinely serve society. With a focus on youth, the Games aim to harness the energy and creativity of the younger generation, making them central to the event's impact.

The motto urges us to recognize that we all have a shared responsibility to tackle today's problems. The Games aspire to showcase the best of France — its boldness, creativity, and innovative spirit. By challenging existing models and paradigms, the organizers aim to bring people together, instill pride, and offer a shared experience beyond conventional expectations.

Chapter 10: Athletes to Watch at the 2024 Olympics

The 2024 Olympics are on the horizon, featuring about 10, 500 athletes across 329 events in 32 sports. The grand opening is set for July 26, 2024, at the iconic Stade de France, with the closing ceremony scheduled for August 11. The enchanting Jardins du Trocadéro and the Seine will host the opening ceremony.

Reflecting on the recently concluded 19th Pan American Games in Santiago, Chile, athletes are now gearing up for the Paris Olympics. For many, the Pan Ams marked their final major championships before the grand stage in Paris, leaving lasting impressions with performances that have earmarked them as ones to watch.

Piper Kelly

Piper Kelly, a 24-year-old sport climber from the United States, seized the women's speed gold in Santiago. Exploiting a false start from compatriot Emma Hunt, Kelly clocked a personal best of 7. 52, showcasing her prowess on the climbing wall.

Fay DeFazio Ebert

In skateboarding, Canada's Fay DeFazio Ebert emerged as a rising star by clinching victory in the women's park competition. Her skill and style hint at a promising future in the world of skateboarding, making her a noteworthy athlete to watch in Paris.

Azura Stevens

Azura Stevens, a 27-year-old former WNBA champion, led Team USA to 3x3 basketball gold in Santiago. With a stellar performance in the final against Colombia, where the Americans triumphed 21-14, Stevens contributed nearly half of the squad's points. As she returns to the Los Angeles Sparks for her seventh

WNBA season in 2024, all eyes are on her potential impact in Paris.

Bill May

After a decade-long retirement, Bill May, a 44-year-old artistic swimmer from the United States, returned to competition at the 2015 World Aquatics Championships. In Santiago, he played a crucial role in lifting his U. S. squad to silver, securing a coveted quota for Paris 2024. For May, competing in Paris would be a dream come true.

Osmar Olvera

Mexico's Osmar Olvera, a 19-year-old diving sensation, dominated the Pan American Games by claiming three golds in 1m springboard, 3m individual springboard, and 3m synchro. Olvera's remarkable performance sets the stage for his journey towards the World Championships qualification and the anticipated Tokyo Olympics.

Felix Dolci

Felix Dolci is a 21-year-old gymnast from Canada. He etched his name in Pan American Games history by becoming the first Canadian man to secure all-around gold since 1963. His prowess extended to floor exercise, contributing to his impressive five-medal haul in Chile.

Mallory Franklin

Great Britain's Mallory Franklin is a successful female canoeist who aims to continue her triumphs in Paris. With a silver in the first Olympic women's C1 race at Tokyo 2020 and the reigning C1 world champion, Franklin is set to contest the kayak cross, making its Games debut in 2024.

Toby Roberts

Nineteen-year-old Toby Roberts made history by becoming the first British man to qualify for climbing at the Olympics. His victory in the European qualifiers in October 2023 solidified his status as a climbing prodigy, coached by his father Tristian and making waves as a vlogger on YouTube and Instagram.

Tom Daley

Tom Daley, a 27-year-old diver from Great Britain, not only secured his first Olympic Gold in the 10m synchro but also claimed a second Bronze for the 10m individual dive. With his dual identity as a diver and YouTube personality, Daley is poised to be a captivating figure in the Great Britain team for Paris 2024.

Simone Biles

Simone Biles, a powerhouse in artistic gymnastics from the USA, faced challenges in Tokyo 2020, winning Silver and Bronze and withdrawing from four finals. Despite the setbacks, the 25-year-old's incredible skills and resilience make her a top contender to shine brightly in Paris 2024.

Naomi Osaka: Tennis Star

Japanese tennis sensation Naomi Osaka, a four-time Grand Slam champion, aims for redemption in the 2024 Olympics after falling short in Tokyo 2020. Despite a third-round exit in Women's singles, Shai's mum's determination and ambitions to win more Grand Slam titles add anticipation to her return to the tennis court in Paris.

Momiji Nishiya and Sky Brown

Momiji Nishiya, a 15-year-old skateboarder from Japan, made history by becoming one of the youngest-ever Olympic Gold medalists in the women's street competition. Similarly, Great Britain's 14-year-old skateboarder Sky Brown secured a Bronze medal in Tokyo. Both prodigies are expected to continue their meteoric rise in the next Olympic Games.

Armand Duplantis

Sweden's Armand Duplantis, a 23-year-old pole vaulter, secured a height of 6. 02m (19 ft 9 in) on his first attempt at Tokyo 2020. After narrowly missing out on beating his own world record, Duplantis remains a pole vaulting phenomenon to watch in the upcoming Olympics in Paris.

Sunisa Lee

At just 19 years old, Sunisa Lee has already secured Gold, Silver, and Bronze Olympic medals in all-around, team, and uneven bars, respectively. Lee, alongside her compatriot Simone Biles, is poised to once again captivate the audience with her exceptional gymnastic prowess in Paris.

Katie Ledecky

Katie Ledecky, a 25-year-old swimming sensation from the USA, added two Golds and two Silvers to the national team's silverware cabinet in the summer's

Olympics. With her remarkable achievements, Ledecky is expected to shine once again in the upcoming Olympics, showcasing her prowess in the pool.

Megumi Field

Trained in ballet, gymnastics, and artistic swimming, Megumi Field stands as the youngest member of the U. S. artistic swimming team. Making her international debut at the age of 11, Field has since won an impressive 22 medals across all disciplines, marking her as a prodigy in the world of artistic swimming.

Jaydin Blackwell

At the age of 19, Jaydin Blackwell emerged as a relative newcomer to the world of elite Para track and field. Making a spectacular debut at the 2023 World Para Athletics Championships in Paris, Blackwell became the world champion in both the men's 100-meter T-38 and men's 400-meter T-38, setting a world record with a time of 48. 49 in the latter.

Erriyon Knighton

Despite being only 19, Erriyon Knighton has been on the pro circuit for over three years. Starting track and field in his high school freshman year, Knighton excelled as a two-sport athlete in both football and track and field. At 18, he broke the under-20 record for the men's 200-meter, a record previously held by Jamaica's Usain Bolt.

Noah Lyles:

How can I forget Noah Lyles?

Noah Lyles was born on July 18, 1997, in Gainesville, Florida. He is a 26-year-old sprinting sensation from the USA who aims for an unexpected quadruple at the Paris 2024 Olympics. The men's 100m and 200m world champion expresses his desire to test himself over a longer distance, participating in the 4x400m relay in addition to his signature events and the 4x100m relay.

Noah Lyles' ambitious pursuit of four gold medals doesn't come out of the blue. As a high school star at the Penn Relays, the Tokyo 2020 bronze medallist showcased his prowess by leading his team from second last to first in the 4x400m relay. Lyles' consideration to extend his repertoire reflects his astonishing period of dominance, having won three consecutive 200m world titles and a triple victory in the last year's world championships.

The stage is set for the 2024 Paris Olympics, where a diverse array of athletes, from seasoned champions to rising stars and prodigies, will converge to showcase their talent, determination, and quest for Olympic glory. As the countdown begins, the world eagerly anticipates the stories that will unfold on the grand stage of Paris 2024.

Conclusion

The journey leading to the 2024 Summer Olympics in Paris has been marked by challenges, triumphs, and the unwavering determination of athletes from around the globe. The bidding process, filled with withdrawals and uncertainties, ultimately paved the way for Paris to shine as the chosen host, a decision solidified during the 131st IOC Session in Lima, Peru.

As we eagerly anticipate the unfolding of this grand event, it's worth noting the comprehensive breakdown of the scheduled events. Paris and its metropolitan region, along with select cities like Lille, Marseille, and even Teahupo'o village in French Polynesia, are gearing up to host a wide array of competitions. From handball tournaments to sailing, football, and even the exotic venue for surfing, the 2024 Olympics promise a richness of sports, culture, and global unity.

With 226 days remaining until the commencement of the Olympics, the excitement is palpable. As your guide through this exciting journey, I, Paul, am committed to keeping you updated on the latest events, breakthroughs, and stories surrounding the 2024 Olympics. This book serves as a snapshot of the events so far, capturing the anticipation and the potential for unforgettable moments in the heart of Paris.

Let the countdown begin, and may the 2024 Summer Olympics in Paris be a celebration of human achievement, strength, and the boundless spirit of competition. Stay tuned for more updates as we inch closer to the spectacle that will undoubtedly etch its legacy in the annals of sporting history.

About the Author

Meet Paul Hiyonder, a skilled author from the United States who specializes in communication and language. Paul loves creating stories and has made a career out of it.

When he's not writing, Paul finds comfort and inspiration in music. He enjoys listening to tunes that touch his soul. Alongside his literary pursuits, Paul likes playing golf for both its strategy and leisure.

Living in the U.S., Paul has always been fascinated by the Olympics. This global sporting event holds a special place in his heart. As a devoted fan, he looks forward to the stories and victories that will unfold during the 2024 Summer Olympics. Join Paul on his journey as he blends his love for language with the excitement of the upcoming Olympic spectacle.

Printed in Great Britain
by Amazon

43211170R00050